WHAT WOULD HAPPEN IF...

ILLNESSES BECAME RESISTANT TO MEDICINE?

Written by Izzi Howell

Illustrated by Paula Bossio

WORLD BOOK

www.worldbook.com

READING TIPS

his book asks readers to ponder the question *what would happen if illnesses became resistant to medicine?* Readers will learn about different illnesses and how they are caused and treated. They will then contemplate what our world would look like if illnesses became resistant to medicine. Use these tips to help readers consider the ripple effects of certain actions and events.

Before Reading

Explain to readers that this book uses cause and effect to show how different illnesses are caused and the important role that medicine plays in peoples' lives around the world. Cause and effect can help us think about why things happen the way they do. It can also help us think about what might happen in the future. Encourage readers to be on the lookout for examples of a cause and effect structure as they explore what would happen if illnesses became resistant to medicine.

During Reading

Discuss with readers how some actions and events have multiple causes and others have multiple effects. Explain that it can be tricky to keep all the if/then scenarios straight in our minds, so it can be helpful to create a visual guide. Encourage readers to draw and add notes to their own cause and effect maps like the one found on pages 20-21.

After Reading

After finishing the book, discuss with readers how their understandings and opinions of different types of illnesses and their treatments have changed. Additionally, you can have readers respond to the comprehension questions included on page 46 and complete the Chain of Events activity on page 47 to further extend the learning.

Visit **www.worldbook.com/resources** for additional, free educational materials.

There is a glossary of terms on pages 44–45. Terms defined in the glossary are in boldface type that **looks like this** on their first appearance on any spread (two facing pages).

Contents

Germs under control?

Achoo! Feeling sick? Illnesses are an unfortunate but unavoidable part of life. And unluckily, there are so many different types, from coughs, colds, and upset stomachs, to more serious infections, such as tuberculosis, and such life-threatening diseases as cancer and heart disease.

Thankfully, we have medicines to fight back! At the very least, medicines can help us feel better a bit sooner. With more serious illnesses, medicines can help save lives.

DID YOU KNOW?

There are around 1 billion cases of the flu around the world every year.

In ancient Greek and Roman times, they used cabbage as medicine!

We now have **vaccines** to prevent over 20 different illnesses.

Heart disease, lung disease, and chest infections are among the top 10 causes of death.

Most people catch **infectious** illnesses from each other, but you can also catch illnesses from animals.

However, doctors have been noticing that some medicines aren't working as well as they used to. Some tiny germs that cause illnesses have become resistant to medicine. This means that they aren't killed off when people take medicine, and so the medicine has no effect.

THINK ABOUT IT!
What do you do to help yourself feel better when you're sick? Do you take medicine or do something else?

I'm not scared of you!

Scientists are warning that germs that cause other diseases may also become resistant to medicines soon. If this happens, we'll have a much bigger problem on our hands! Let's take a look at what would happen if illnesses became resistant to medicine.

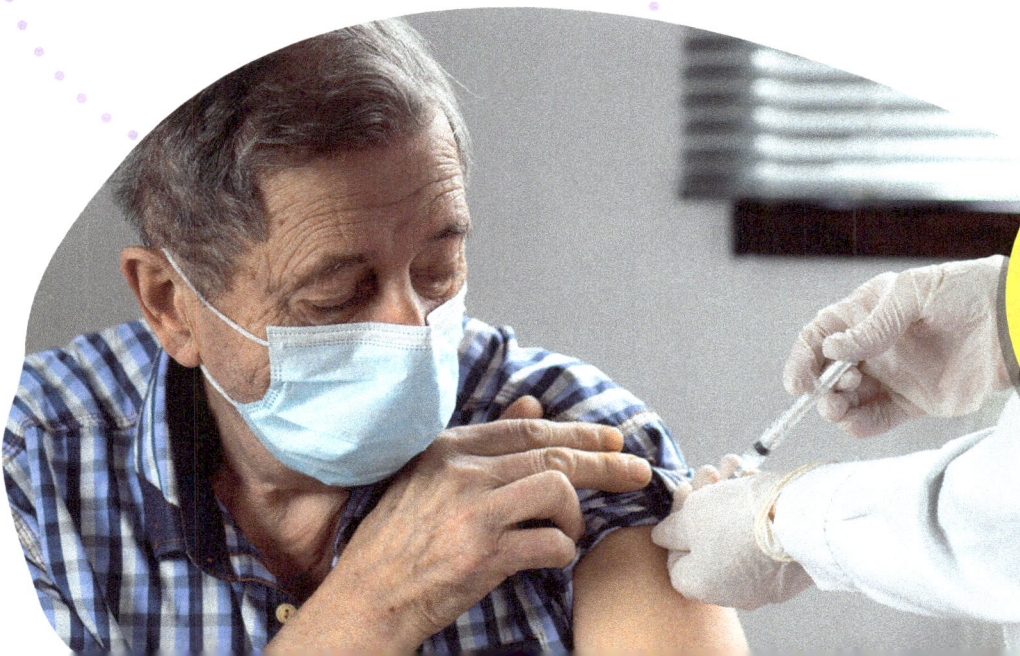

This man is receiving a flu vaccine. Vaccines have an important role to play in keeping illnesses from becoming **drug-resistant**.

5

Illness info

An illness is any disease that affects the body or the mind. We often split illnesses into different categories depending on what causes them. **Infectious** diseases happen when germs enter your body and start reproducing inside. **Noninfectious** diseases aren't caused by germs.

There are several different types of germs (or **pathogens,** if you want to use the correct scientific name!)—**bacteria, viruses, fungi,** and other tiny living things. Nearly all of them are far too small for us to see with the naked eye.

Bacteria are simple living things made up of just one **cell.** Cells are the building blocks that all living things are made up of.

Fungi are a type of small living thing. They can be single-celled or made up of lots of cells.

Protozoans are single-celled living things that are larger and more complex than bacteria.

Viruses are even simpler and smaller than bacteria, and they aren't technically "alive." They aren't made of cells—they are made up of particles instead—but they can **evolve** and change like living things.

Worms (yes, worms—yuck!) can cause illnesses if they enter the body.

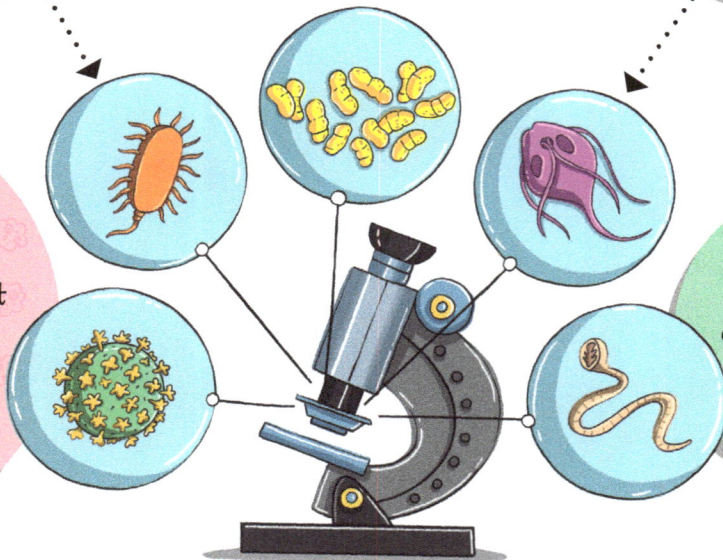

BACTERIA

Bacteria are one of the most widespread living things on Earth. They are found almost everywhere—in the air, in the soil, in water, and in your body! Luckily for us, most of these bacteria are harmless. In fact, many of them are actually very useful. Bacteria help us make cheese and yogurt, process sewage, digest food, and can even protect us against other infections.

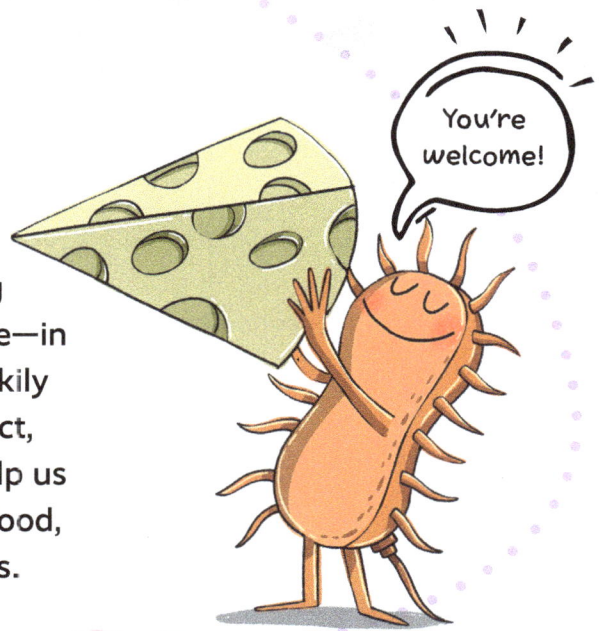

You're welcome!

However, there are a few bad bacteria that will make you sick if they get inside your body. They often cause infections on your skin and in your throat, lungs, or stomach. They are also responsible for such diseases as tuberculosis, strep throat, and some types of meningitis and pneumonia.

DID YOU KNOW?
To **reproduce**, a bacterial cell splits itself into two.

Pimples are also caused by bacteria!

FUN FACT!
There are 10 times more bacterial cells in your body than human cells!

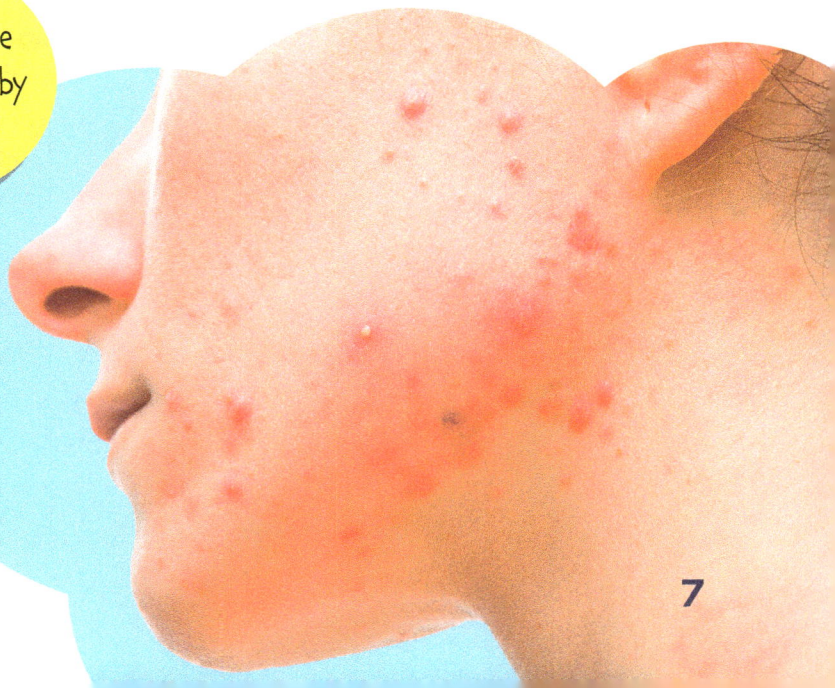

VIRUSES

Viruses are responsible for many common illnesses including colds, the flu, chickenpox, and measles, as well as more serious diseases, such as HIV/AIDS, polio, and hepatitis.

Viruses are so tiny that they can get inside the **cells** that make up the human body. Most viruses only target certain cells. For example, the flu virus only infects the cells found in our airways and lungs. Once a virus is inside a cell, it reprograms the cell to help it **reproduce** and make more viruses. This process damages or destroys our cells.

FUN FACT! Viruses can only reproduce inside the cells of a living thing! Once they are out of a living body's cells, they won't survive for long.

Nooooo! I can't make it on my own!

FUNGI

Many **fungi** are totally harmless, like the mushrooms in your dinner. However, some fungi aren't quite as friendly! Common fungal illnesses include such minor skin infections as athlete's foot and ringworm. However, people with weakened **immune systems** (see pages 12–15) are at risk of dangerous fungal infections that can spread across their entire body.

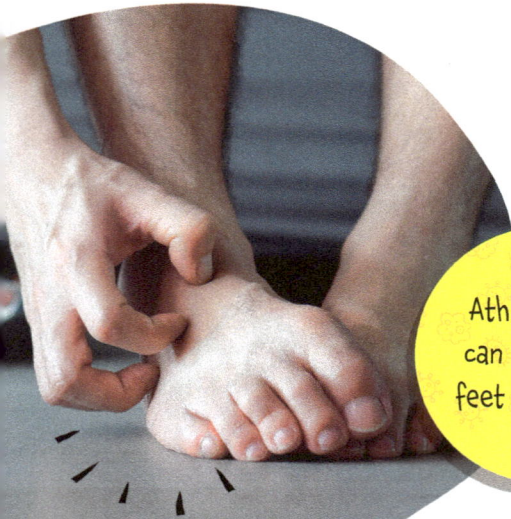

Athlete's foot can make your feet very itchy!

PROTOZOANS

You might not have heard of **protozoans** before, but they are responsible for one of the most widespread serious illnesses—malaria. The protozoans that cause malaria are spread from person to person via infected mosquito bites. They are **parasites** that invade the human body and attack red blood cells.

People in Malawi line up for medicine to treat malaria. Even though there are **drugs** to prevent and treat malaria, many people in less-developed countries don't have access to them or can't afford them.

DID YOU KNOW?
Nearly half of the world's population is at risk of catching malaria.

WORMS

It's not a pleasant thought, but worms can get inside your body and make you sick. Tapeworms set up home in your intestines, where they steal nutrients from the food you are digesting! This can make you hungrier than usual. In tropical areas, tiny worms can cause a serious condition called elephantiasis, in which your arms, legs, and other parts of the body swell up painfully.

Thanks for the banana, buddy!

9

NONINFECTIOUS DISEASES

Cancer, diabetes, heart disease, and arthritis are all **noninfectious** diseases. They aren't caused by **pathogens** and therefore can't spread between people in the air or via surfaces.

Many noninfectious diseases are connected to lifestyle. You are more likely to develop them if you smoke, eat an unhealthy diet, or don't do enough exercise. Some are also linked to aging or the environment. Breathing in pollution regularly or being exposed to dangerous chemicals can damage your body and cause illness.

FUN FACT!

Exercise has been proven to help prevent such illnesses as heart disease and diabetes, as well as boost your mood and improve your mental health!

Some diseases can be **inherited** via the **genes** that you get from your parents. Genes control how your body is built, for example, your hair color or your height. They are found in **cells.** Some people have one gene that doesn't work properly. This can lead to problems with how their body works. This is known as a genetic disease.

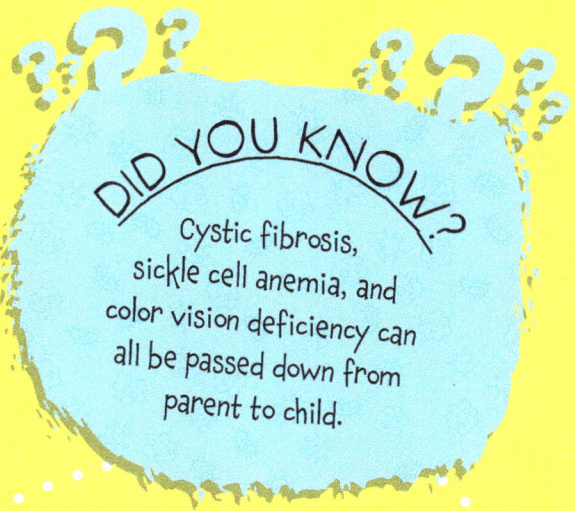

Humans aren't the only living things that can get sick. Animals and plants can catch illnesses, too! Animal and plant diseases can cause big problems. If a large number of living things in an ecosystem catch an illness and die, it can have a massive domino effect on the other living things that depend on them for food. Illnesses that affect crops can also threaten our food supply.

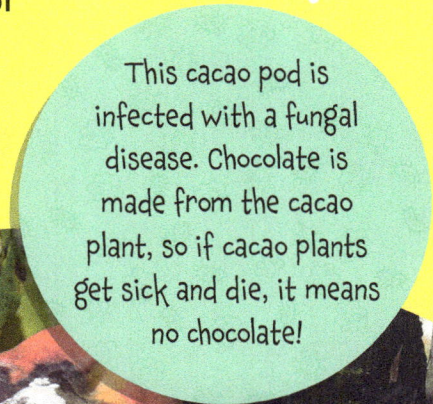

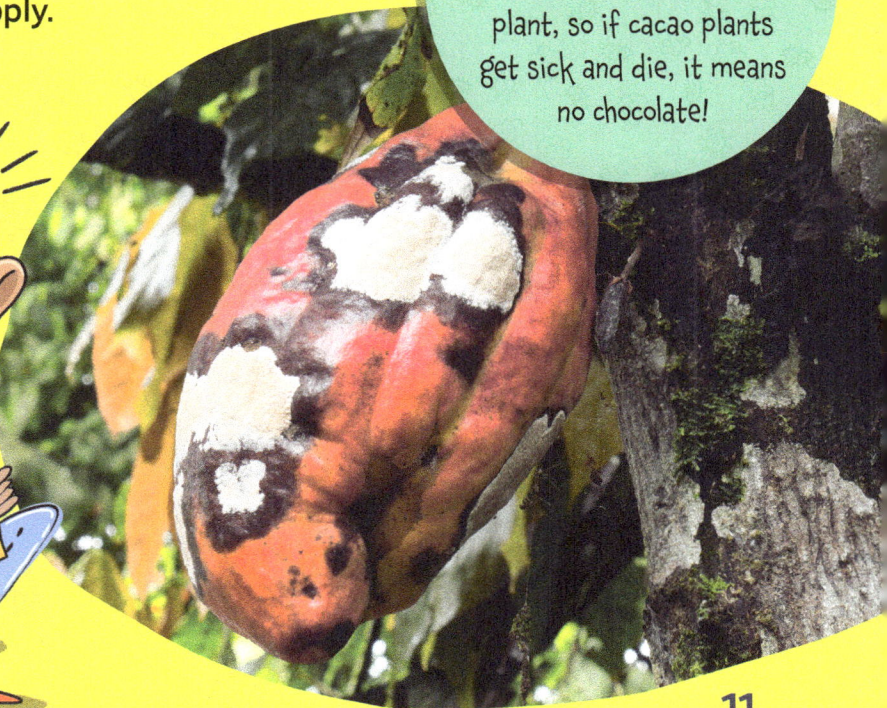

This cacao pod is infected with a fungal disease. Chocolate is made from the cacao plant, so if cacao plants get sick and die, it means no chocolate!

Mighty medicine

For most of human history, we didn't have very effective ways to treat illnesses. Scientists didn't know what caused these conditions or how to make medicines to cure them. Many people died from illnesses as a result.

Aside from simple herbal treatments, we only had our **immune systems** to protect us from disease. Our immune system is our body's way of protecting itself from sickness, much like a country's army defends it from attack.

The immune system is made up of many different body parts and specialized **cells** that work together. Mucus and tiny hairlike cells in your nose and throat trap and sweep germs out of your airways. Superstrong acid in your stomach kills many harmful **pathogens.** However, some germs will find a way through into your bloodstream. That's when it's time for the major immune superheroes—white blood cells!

FUN FACT! Your tears contain germ-busting chemicals that protect your eyes from infections!

White blood cells make chemicals called **antibodies** that recognize and fight against germs that enter the body. Once your body has learned how to make the right antibodies to kill one type of germ, it can make them again very quickly and easily in some cases. If this type of germ gets into your body again, you won't get sick because your body can immediately produce antibodies to wipe it out. This is called **immunity.**

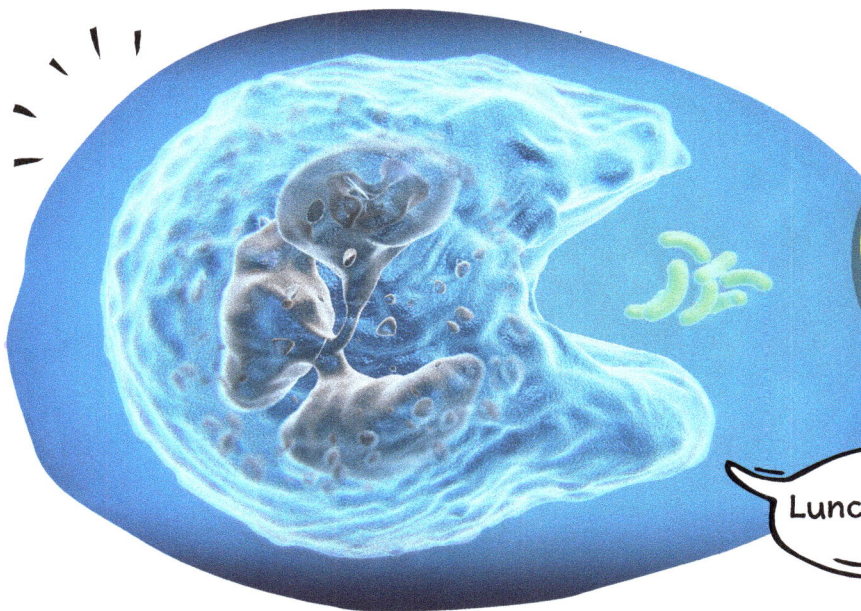

White blood cells can also surround germs and kill them directly.

Lunchtime!

Our **immune system** can cope with many minor illnesses. However, sometimes it needs help. That's where medicines and **vaccines** come in to play.

The type of medicine needed to treat an illness depends on the type of germ that causes the illness. Medicines for **infectious** illnesses are designed to kill certain **pathogens** and stop them from reproducing. If you take the wrong type of medicine, it won't work! So **antibiotics** will only work on **bacteria**, antifungals will only kill **fungi,** and so on.

TYPE OF GERM	ILLNESSES CAUSED	MEDICINE NEEDED
Bacteria	Tuberculosis, strep throat, whooping cough	Antibiotic
Viruses	The flu, colds, COVID-19, chickenpox, measles, HIV/AIDS	Antiviral
Fungi	Athlete's foot, ringworm, thrush	Antifungal
Protozoans	Malaria, toxoplasmosis, giardia	Antiprotozoal
Worms	Tapeworms, elephantiasis	Antiparasitic

THINK ABOUT IT!

Sometimes people ask doctors for antibiotics to treat their cold or the flu. Why won't antibiotics help them feel better?

I still feel terrible!

Vaccines are medicines that can prevent infectious diseases by giving you **immunity** against them (see page 13). Some vaccines contain dead or weakened germs. Exposure to these germs teaches your immune system how to make **antibodies** to fight them without your body actually becoming ill. Other vaccines use parts of pathogens or genetic material from pathogens to create a response in your immune system to protect you from the sickness.

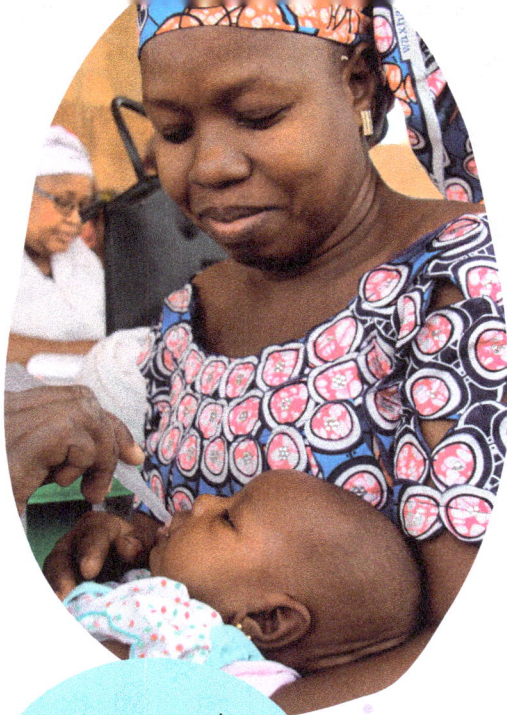

Vaccines can be placed in the mouth, like the vaccine for polio shown here, or given as an injection.

FUN FACT!

Vaccines prevent between 3.5 and 5 million deaths every year!

There are also medicines to help control and cure **noninfectious** diseases. They can reduce the effects of the illness and keep it from harming your body. For example, people with diabetes often take the medicine insulin to control their blood sugar levels. Without this medicine, diabetes can result in lots of harm to the body, including nerve damage, vision problems, and kidney failure.

People with diabetes can now use insulin pumps to automatically monitor and deliver insulin into their body.

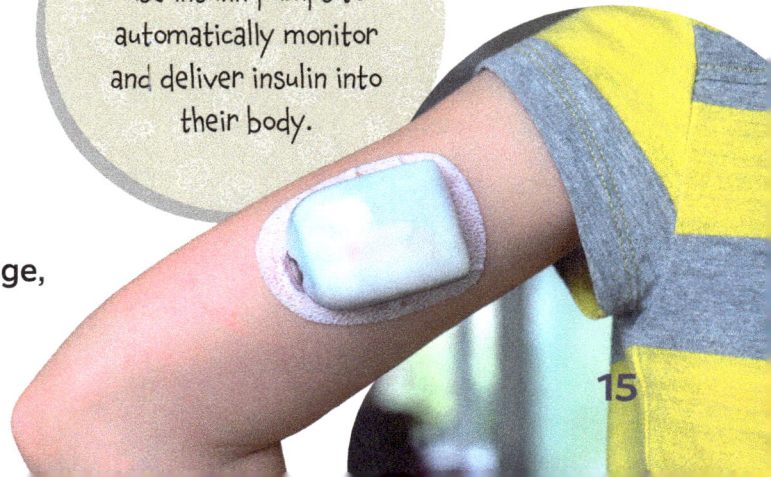

15

All the medicines that we have today are the result of years and years of scientists' hard work. They have developed **vaccines,** treatments, and cures for many diseases that used to kill huge numbers of people. We've even been able to use these vaccines to entirely wipe out the devastating disease smallpox. The World Health Organization hopes it will eventually be able to eradicate other diseases, including malaria and polio.

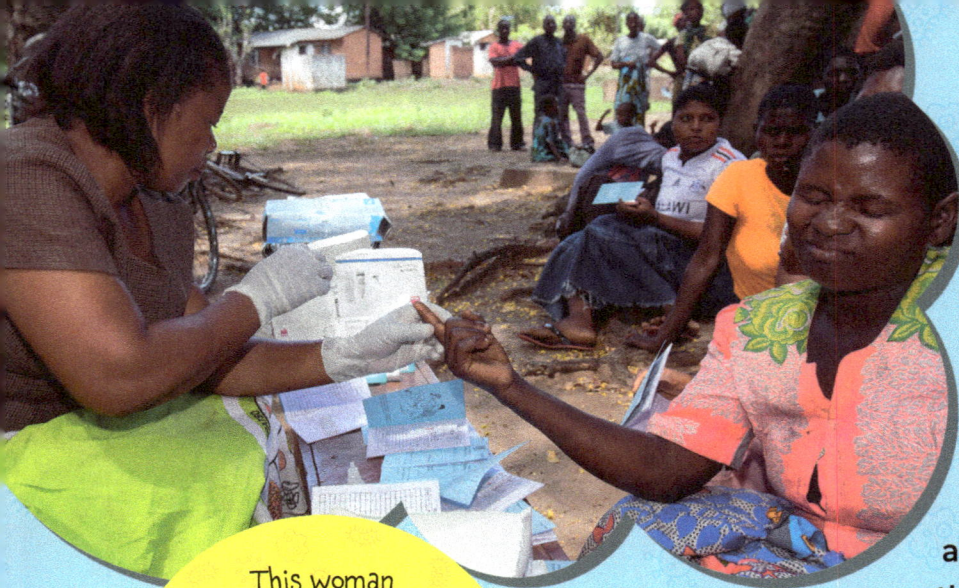

This woman in Malawi is being tested for malaria. Testing for and treating malaria as quickly as possible is key if we want to eradicate it.

FUN FACT!

Smallpox has been officially eradicated since 1980!

THINK ABOUT IT!

What do you think it would have been like to live at a time before medicines and vaccines were widely available in many places?

When new diseases appear, such as COVID-19, scientists race to create vaccines and more effective medicines to treat them. These treatments prevent serious illness and death, and they can also help slow down the spread of the disease.

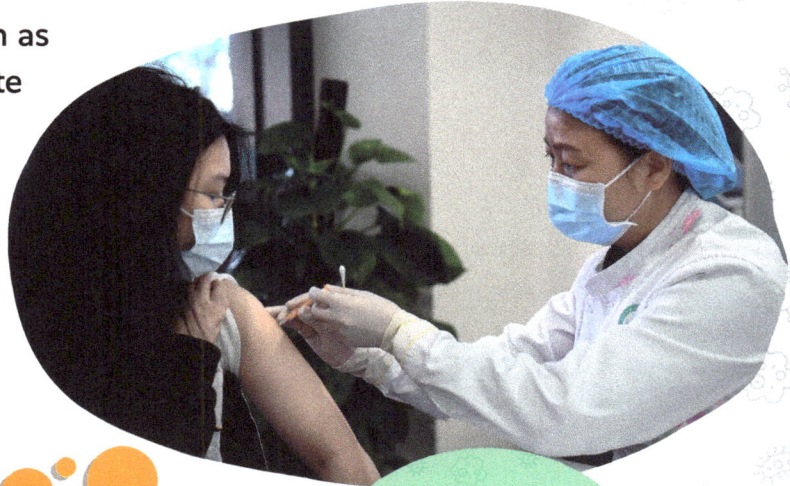

It's estimated that COVID-19 vaccines prevented almost 20 million deaths in the first year that they were available.

Hi! I'm Uğur Şahin. I'm a scientist and founder of BioNTech, which helped develop the first major COVID-19 vaccine. Before the COVID-19 **pandemic,** my team were researching how to use genetic material to fight against cancer. We quickly switched to working on a COVID-19 vaccine. We used techniques from our previous research to develop a vaccine that uses genetic material to instruct the body's own **cells** to make chemicals that protect it from COVID-19. It's important for scientists to have an open mind, since ideas and techniques can often be used in many different ways!

Oh, interesting! That gives me an idea ...

Ever since the discovery of **drug**-resistant illnesses, scientists have been working hard to develop new medicines to treat them. However, they're struggling to keep up as germs become resistant at ever-increasing speeds. This is due to many different activities that make it more likely for germs to develop resistance. Turn the page to find out more!

17

Becoming resistant

Scientists have noticed that some medicines aren't working as effectively as they used to against **infectious** illnesses. This is because the germs that cause the diseases are able to **mutate** and **evolve** so that they aren't affected by a certain medicine. Super clever, but very annoying! Let's find out how and why this happens.

Most **pathogens,** including **bacteria, fungi, protozoans,** and worms, are living things. Like all living things, pathogens experience random genetic changes. If one of these changes benefits the pathogen and makes it easier for the pathogen to survive, it's more likely that the pathogen will live long enough to **reproduce** and pass on its genetic advantage to other pathogens. Little by little, this change will spread among all the pathogens until they all have the same advantage. This is known as evolution.

Some germs can even change so that they aren't affected by lots of different types of medicine!

Check me out!

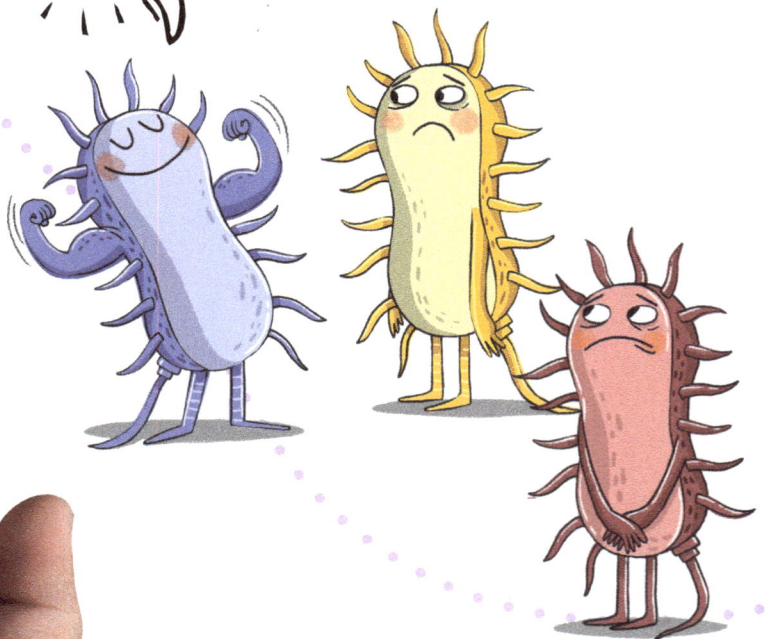

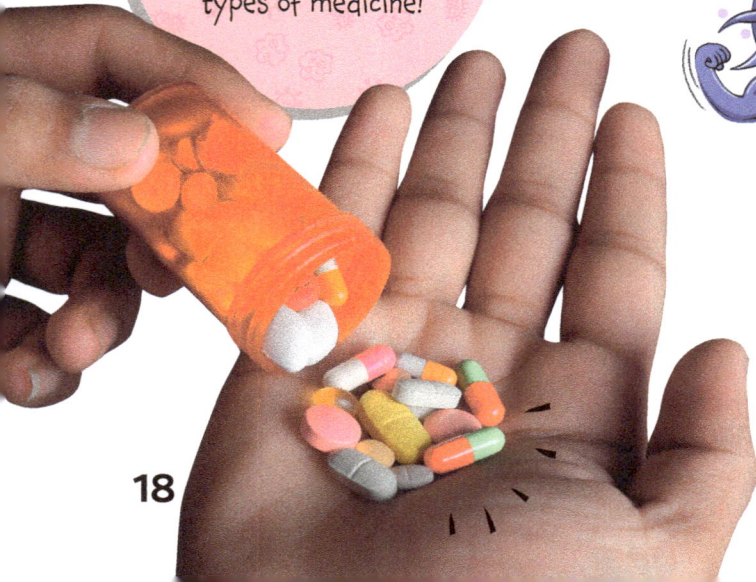

18

THINK ABOUT IT!

If you could mutate to have a fun or powerful genetic advantage, what would it be, and why?

FUN FACT!

Viruses aren't technically living things, but they can mutate and evolve just like living things!

When pathogens come into contact with medicine used to kill them, such as **antibiotics** or **antivirals,** all of the pathogens should be killed. However, if any of the pathogens have a mutation that means they aren't affected by the medicine, they will survive. These pathogens will go on to reproduce and possibly infect other people, passing on the resistant form of the pathogen. **Drug**-resistant pathogens are sometimes known as **superbugs.**

Drug-resistant illnesses can make people very sick, since it's much harder to find treatments that can kill the germs that cause them.

DID YOU KNOW?

Around 1.3 million people die every year because of antibiotic resistance.

Some amount of **drug** resistance was always going to develop in germs, because it's a natural process. However, there are many factors that are making it happen faster and more often. A lot of them relate to how we use (or misuse!) medicine.

How does medicine use lead to drug resistance?

Doctors and other health care professionals prescribe the wrong type of medicine, for example, **antibiotics** are given to treat a cold (which is a viral infection).

Germs are unnecessarily exposed to medicine. The medicine will kill most germs, leaving behind any that are naturally drug resistant. These germs will survive to **reproduce,** passing along their resistance to other germs.

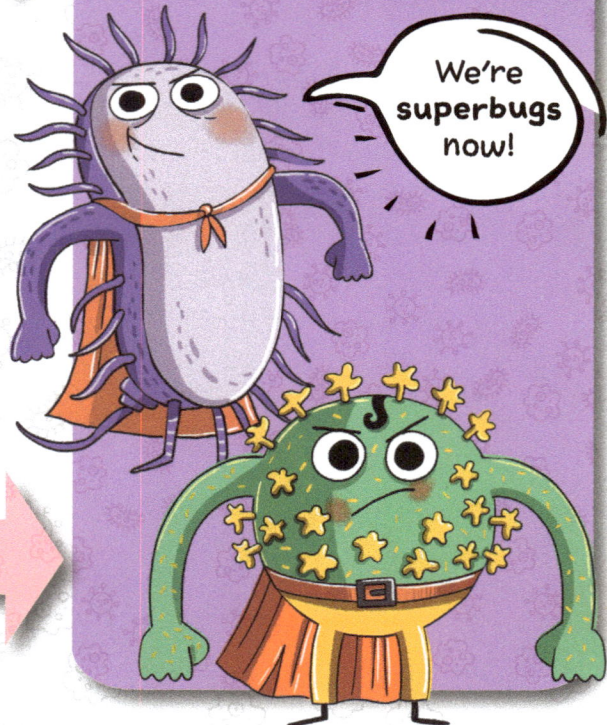

We're **superbugs** now!

Many people around the world don't have access to **vaccines** that protect them against common but serious infections, such as tuberculosis. They are much more likely to catch these diseases, which then will need to be treated with medicine.

Doctors and other health care professionals prescribe medicine that isn't necessary, for example, to treat a very minor infection that the body's **immune system** could handle by itself.

I can take you, no problem!

People self-medicate with old medicines or medicines from family members. They give themselves the wrong dose or wrong drugs to treat their infection.

Let's see if this works.

People don't take the full course of treatment for an infection. If you stop before the end of the treatment, not all germs will have been killed. Some stronger germs may be left behind.

Doctors don't prescribe specialized medicines designed to kill specific germs, since they don't have access to the medicines or don't want to spend time identifying the germs in a laboratory. More general medicines aren't as effective, so some germs remain in the body.

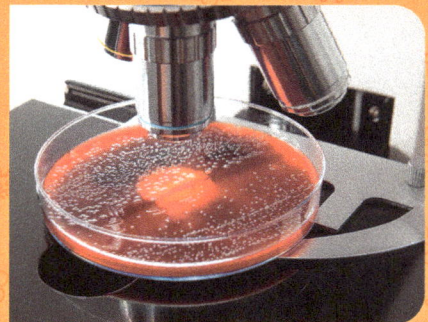

Incorrect use of medicine isn't the only way that germs become resistant to **drugs** or that drug-resistant illnesses spread. Scientists have discovered many other issues that contribute to the problem, including lack of health care and poor **sanitation.**

Drug-resistant germs have already spread to most parts of the world, including many less-developed countries. When people in these areas become sick, they may not have the money or opportunity to receive any kind of medicine, let alone the special treatments needed for drug-resistant illnesses. With no treatment, illnesses spread fast from person to person.

What's more, some countries don't have the money or **infrastructure** to deal with waste properly. It pollutes rivers, lakes, and farms where food is grown. When people use and drink polluted water and eat food grown in polluted soil, it exposes them to many **pathogens,** making it more likely for them to become ill. Germs from sick people's waste are also spread in this way.

People in Bangladesh walk through polluted floodwaters to collect clean drinking water.

DID YOU KNOW?
Two billion people around the world don't have access to a clean, close source of drinking water.

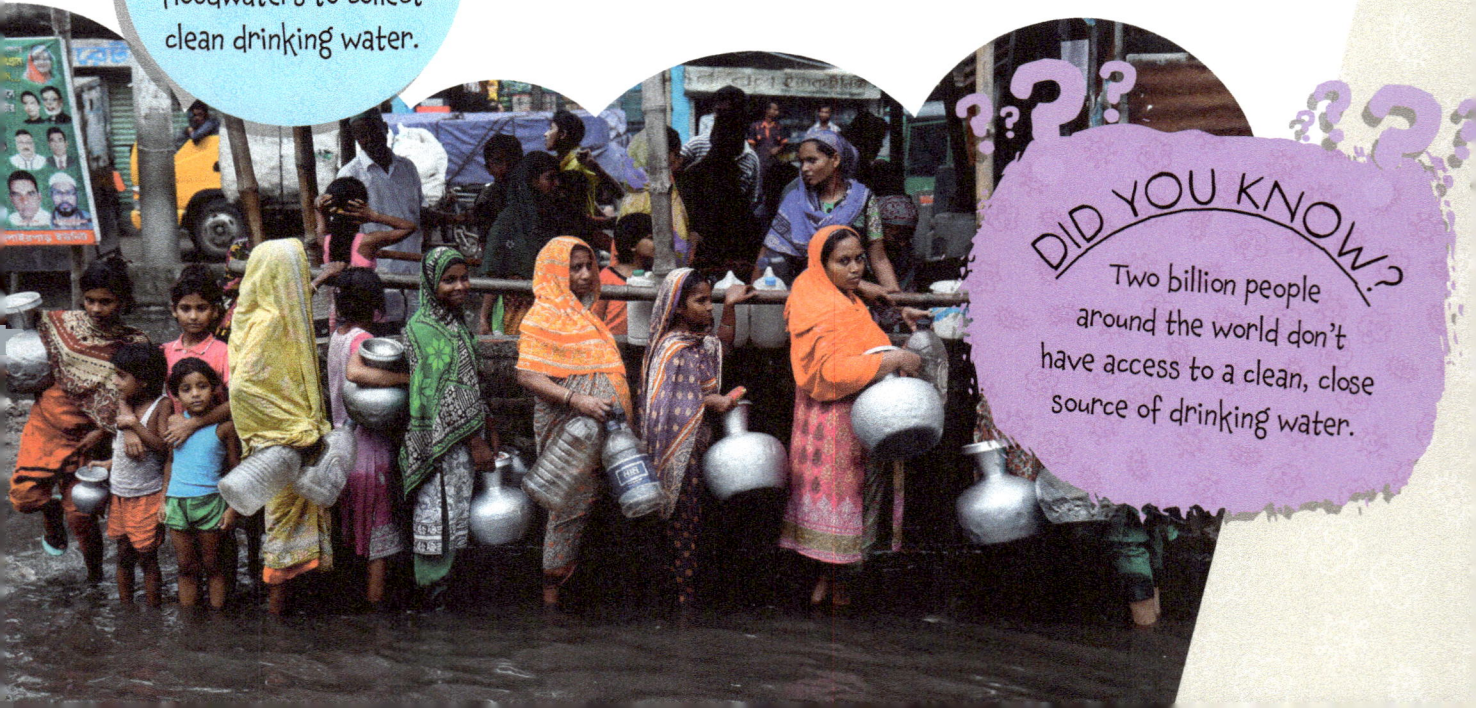

Farmers often give medicine to livestock to keep them from becoming ill (even when they aren't actually sick!). Farmers lose a lot of money if their animals get sick, because they can't sell their meat or any other animal products. This gives germs in the animals' bodies the chance to **mutate** and become drug resistant. These germs can spread to humans through poor **hygiene** or if animal waste isn't treated properly.

Illnesses spread quickly among livestock that are kept close together in small barns.

DID YOU KNOW?

Eating meat or drinking milk from an animal that carries drug-resistant germs can infect you with the same drug-resistant germs.

23

A world without medicine

For now, just a few **infectious** diseases have **mutated** and developed significant resistance to standard medicines. But if we don't address the issues we looked at in the previous chapter, more and more illnesses may follow in their footsteps. What would our world look like if all infectious diseases became resistant to medicine?

THINK ABOUT IT!

Before you read this chapter, write down some predictions as to what a world without medicine would look like. Check back once you've finished the chapter—how many did you guess?

Without medicines, our main weapon against infectious diseases would be our own **immune systems,** which, as we've seen, can only handle so much by themselves! We'd have no treatments to quickly clear up less serious infections, such as ear infections or skin infections.

Even a minor cut can cause a big problem if pesky germs get inside!

We'd also see many more patients dying from more serious infections like pneumonia. Today, with the help of medicine, most pneumonia patients recover, but before antibiotics were developed in the 1940's, pneumonia killed about a third of those who caught it.

Maybe if I rub it on me ...?

This may not seem like a big deal, but if these issues are left untreated, they can result in long-term damage as well as lots of unnecessary pain. In some cases, the infection could even spread throughout your body and turn into a extreme, life-threatening disease called sepsis.

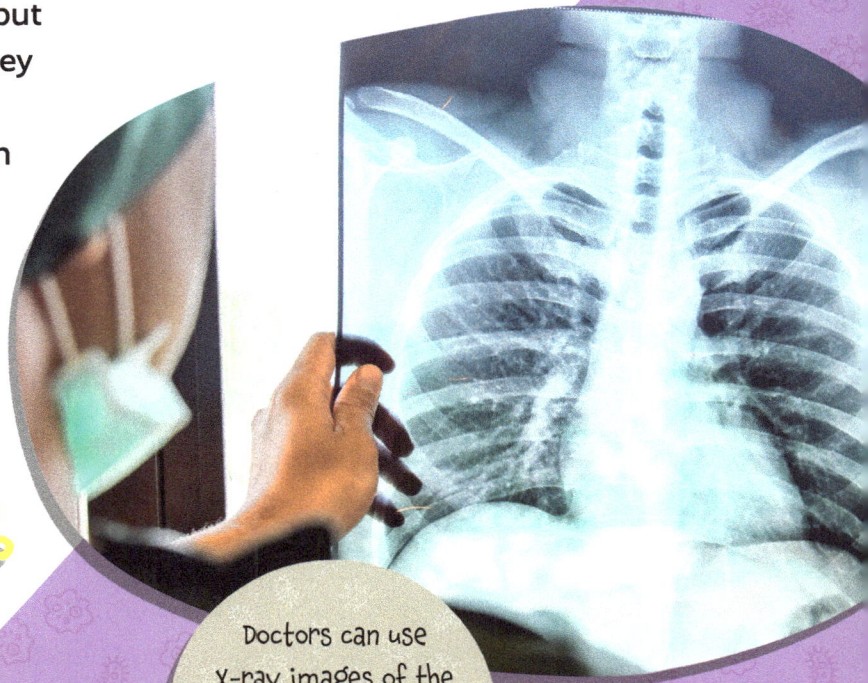

Doctors can use X-ray images of the lungs to confirm if a patient has pneumonia.

The loss of medicine would result in many more deaths from HIV/AIDS. When this disease first became widespread in the 1980's and 1990's, most people who caught it died. People didn't understand how to prevent the spread of HIV/AIDS, and we had very limited ways of treating it.

However, in the past few decades, new **antiviral** medicines have saved the lives of huge numbers of HIV-positive people. HIV is no longer a life-threatening disease, because antiviral **drugs** can keep it from turning into AIDS—the final and most dangerous stage of the disease. If the virus that causes HIV/AIDS became resistant to these treatments, we'd be almost back where we started. Even though we have much better awareness of how to avoid catching HIV, we'd have no methods of treating people who did catch it.

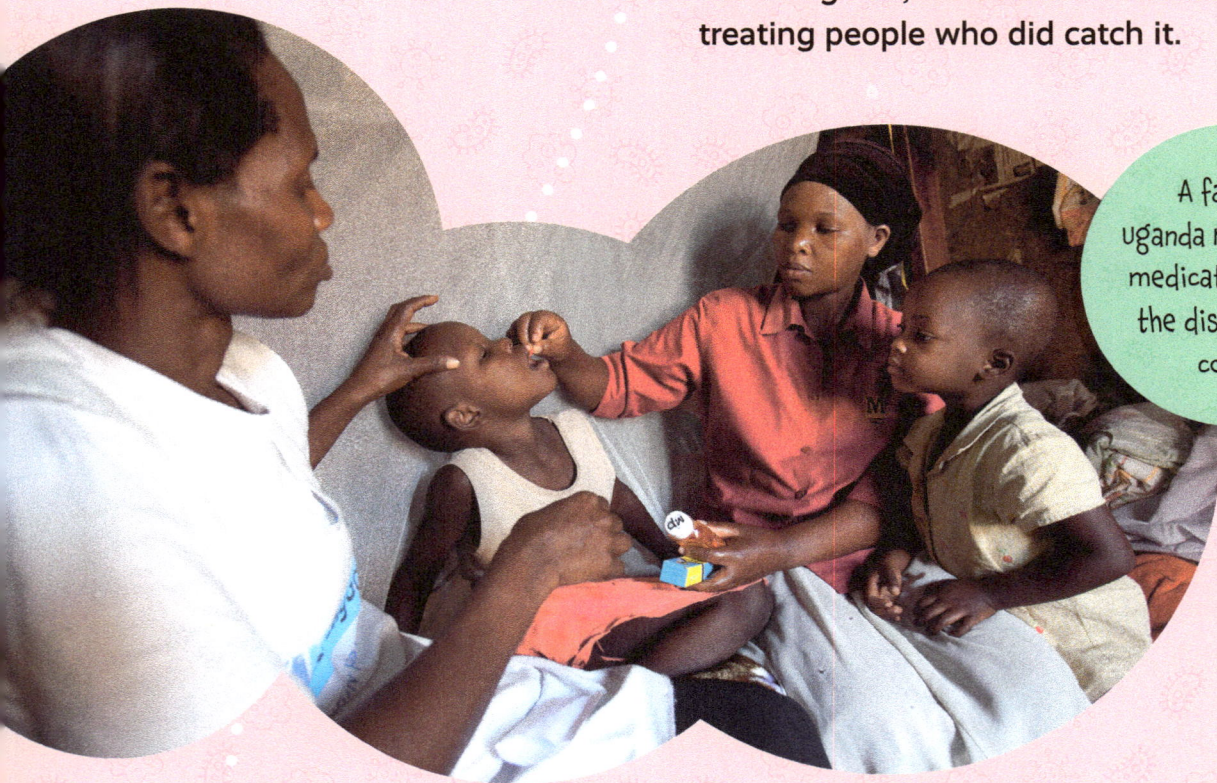

A family in Uganda receives HIV medication to keep the disease under control.

A world without medicine would also be a huge threat to cancer patients undergoing chemotherapy. This treatment is **toxic** to cancer **cells,** but also to the cells in your body, which weakens your **immune system.** This means that it's much harder for cancer patients to fight off even very minor infections.

Many other medical procedures would also become more dangerous without medicine to kill germs. Dental treatments, operations, and childbirth are just a few situations where patients are left with wounds where germs could enter, which puts them at risk of infection. These infections can become very nasty—and even fatal if left untreated.

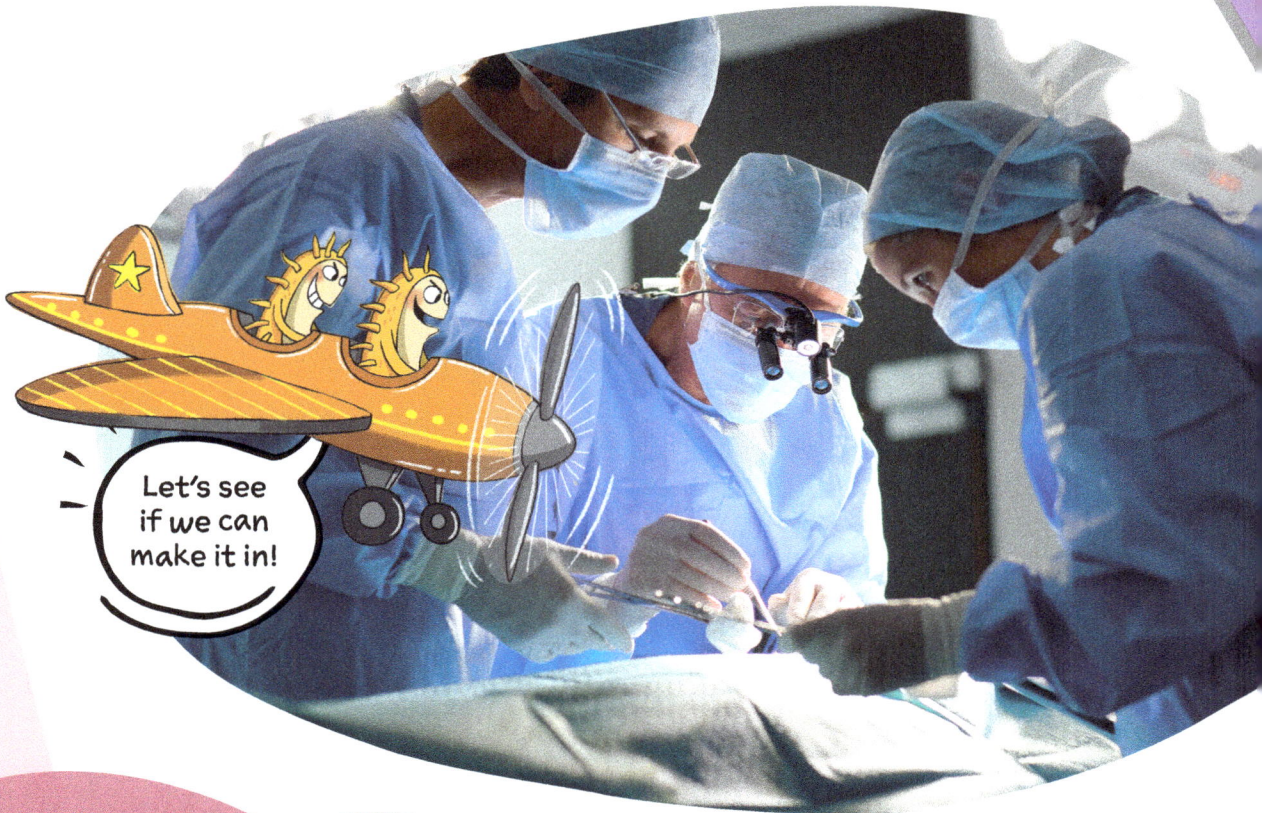

Let's see if we can make it in!

THINK ABOUT IT!

How would your life change if you knew you might catch a dangerous infection if you hurt yourself? Are there any activities you would stop doing?

27

OK, so medicines are gone. At least we still have **vaccines,** right? Well, not necessarily. **Infectious** diseases could also **mutate** to become so different that current vaccines won't work to prevent them. Without vaccines, we would see the return of many life-threatening infectious diseases that are currently under control in many areas, such as tuberculosis.

This child in Malaysia is being vaccinated against tuberculosis.

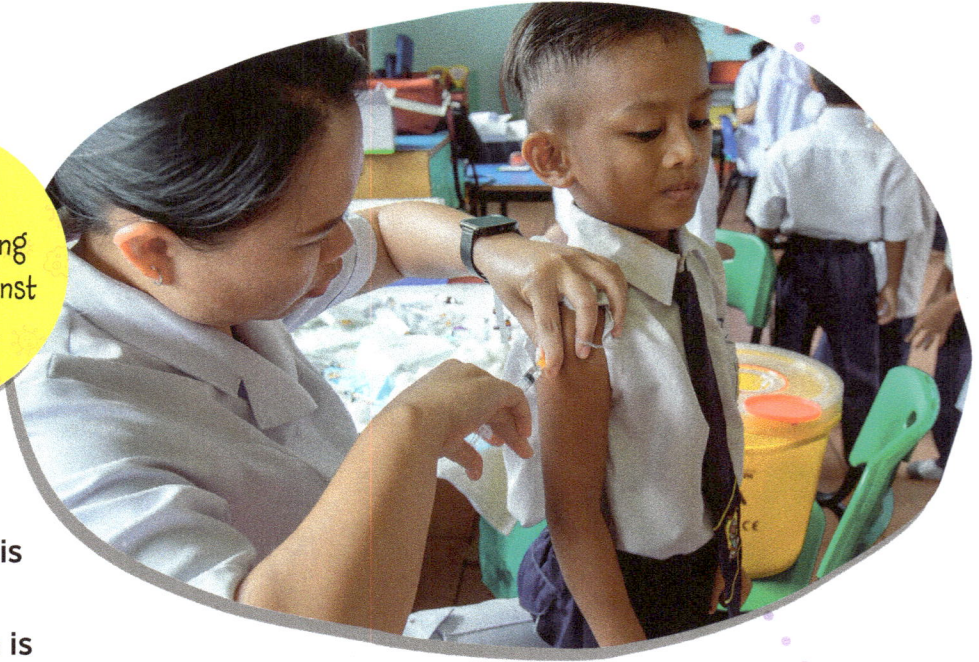

In the past, tuberculosis killed huge numbers of people. The disease is spread through the air, so cases were particularly high in crowded places where people lived close together. Today, many people live in cities, so it's likely that tuberculosis would become a problem there once more. And without vaccines to prevent the disease or medicine to treat it, death rates from tuberculosis could soar once again.

DID YOU KNOW?

Between 1600 and 1800, tuberculosis was responsible for one-quarter of all deaths in Europe.

There are still many cases of the flu every year because it's so contagious, but thanks to vaccines, it's no longer the major threat it once was. Before vaccines were available, there were many flu **pandemics,** which resulted in many deaths. Flu vaccines are used to protect the most vulnerable people, including the elderly, young children, and those with weakened **immune systems.** These people would be most at risk of dying of the flu if they were to catch it.

If the flu vaccine no longer worked, the flu would become a major threat to many people around the world once more. And because the flu is so easy to spread and catch, it's likely that we'd eventually experience another flu pandemic.

DID YOU KNOW? The Spanish flu pandemic (1918–1919) was the deadliest flu pandemic in history, killing about 20 to 50 million people worldwide.

This is an emergency hospital in the United States set up to care for patients during the Spanish flu pandemic.

Ready for some good news? Even if we lost all medicines and **vaccines** for **infectious** illnesses, modern scientific knowledge would not be lost. We know so much more about what causes diseases, how they spread, and how to stop them than scientists of the past.

Yuck!

We live in a much more hygienic world than ever before. Most places have toilets, clean drinking water, and ways to dispose of garbage. People understand the importance of washing their hands, and storing and preparing food correctly. These small things make a huge difference in keeping people from catching infectious diseases in the first place.

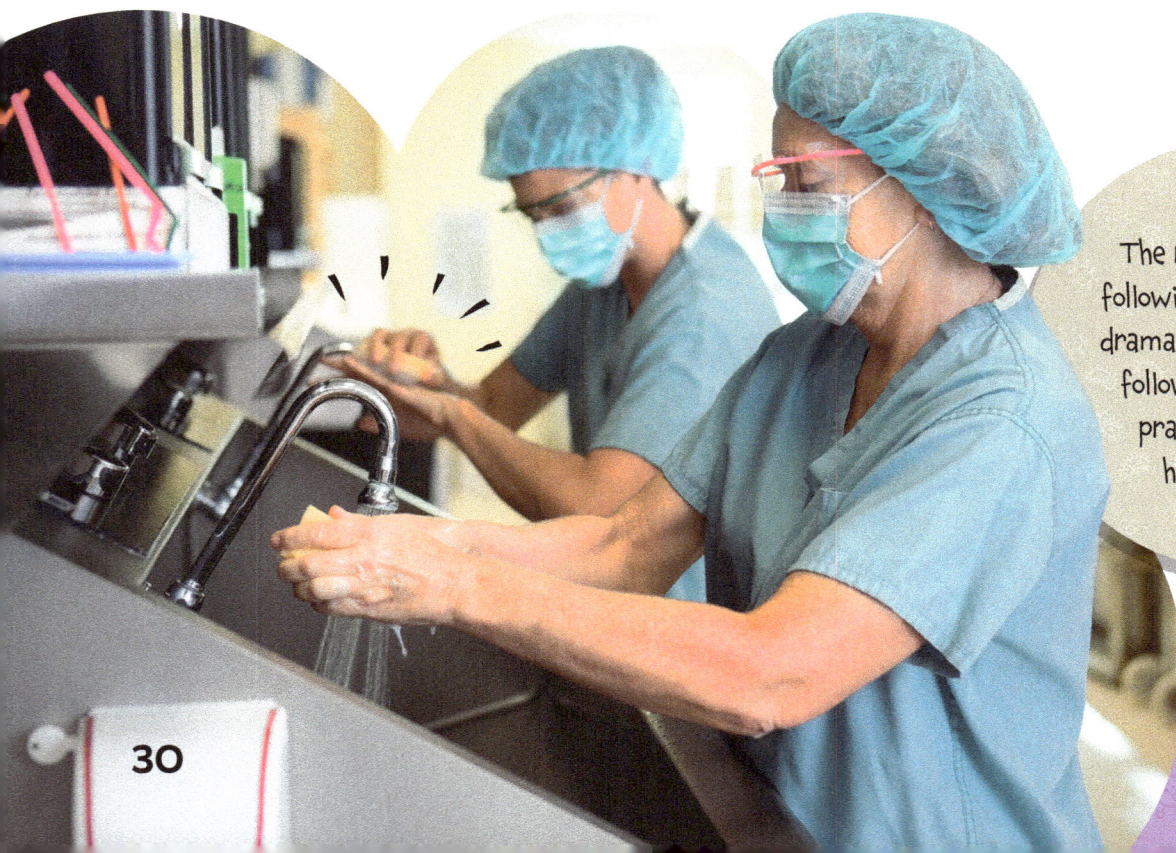

The risk of infection following surgery drops dramatically when staff follow good **hygiene** practices, such as handwashing.

We also know how to control infectious diseases once they occur. Avoiding enclosed spaces and the use of masks can prevent **airborne** diseases from spreading. Regular cleaning kills germs that gather on surfaces. Properly disposing of waste and only drinking clean water reduces the risk of diseases that live in water.

Surfaces that get touched by many people, such as door handles, get much dirtier than you'd think!

What's more, a global network of scientists would be ready to start from scratch and find new medicines and treatments to replace those that were lost. This wouldn't happen overnight, but within a few years, **drug** companies would hopefully be ready to launch new medicines and vaccines to get drug-resistant germs under control.

Hi! I'm Despoina Mavridou. I'm a scientist who studies **bacteria**. My team and I have discovered a way to make **antibiotic**-resistant bacteria vulnerable to antibiotics again. It isn't suitable for use on humans yet, but we're working on that next! When we figure this out, it will be a very valuable weapon in the fight against antibiotic resistance.

We did it!

31

Other diseases

But wait … what about **noninfectious** illnesses? Is there a chance they might become resistant to medicine, too?

The short answer is no, thankfully! These illnesses aren't caused by living **pathogens,** so they can't change and **evolve** to become resistant to medicine. A noninfectious illness is just a direct change that affects a different part or process in your body, for example, your heart rate or how your pancreas works. These conditions are caused by many factors, such as your lifestyle and environment (see pages 10–11 for a recap!).

Only the car exhaust is to blame!

However, there are a few exceptions. For example, certain types of cancer can become resistant to medicines commonly used by doctors. This makes them harder to treat. Most of the time, cancer patients can switch to other **drugs** that the cancer isn't resistant to. This isn't a big risk to the public, unlike drug-resistant **infectious** diseases, because you can't catch cancer from another person. It's a random issue that doctors can often resolve as it occurs. Scientists are also studying this problem to see if they can find more effective treatments that cancer can't become resistant to.

DID YOU KNOW?

If cancer is found and treated early, it's much less likely to become resistant to treatment. This is one of many reasons why it's important to know the warning signs of cancer and go to the doctor if you are concerned!

Keep an eye on any moles that change size, shape, or color—this can be a warning sign of skin cancer.

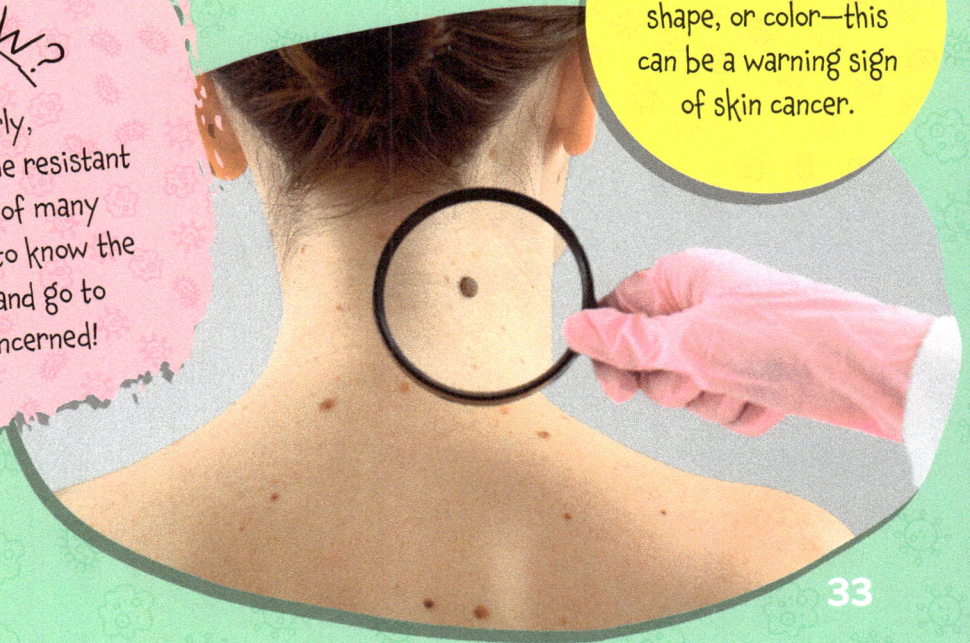

Fighting back!

A world without medicine would be very scary. Luckily, there are lots of things that we can do (and are already doing!) to keep us from getting to that point. Everyone has a part to play in the fight against **drug**-resistant germs, from normal people like you, to doctors and nurses, and governments that pass laws.

Doctors must be careful to only prescribe certain medicines when needed, and if possible, should give specialized medicines rather than general ones. As we've already seen, giving patients medicines for the wrong type of illness can seriously backfire. Not only do these medicines not help you feel better, putting them in your body unnecessarily gives **pathogens** an opportunity to **mutate** and become resistant to them.

Only take medicine that has been prescribed for you (and always take the full course of treatment!).

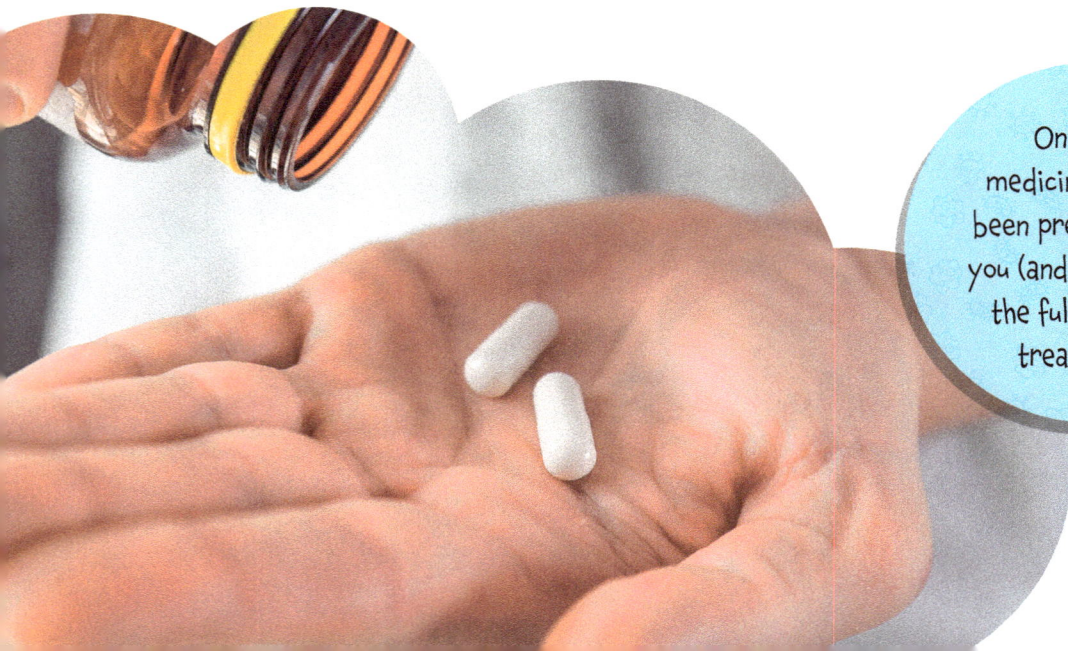

It's just a cold! No antibiotics for you!

An antibiotic? For a **virus** like me? Useless!

Hi! I'm Hong Chen. I'm a scientist who studies how the environment affects people's health. I've recently been working on a research project to prove that air pollution can make antibiotic resistance worse! Our next step is to understand why. One idea is that antibiotic-resistant **bacteria** might be carried in tiny particles of air pollution. Whatever the reason, it's clear that we need to improve air quality to protect people's health.

Making sure you are up to date with **vaccines** is another important way of helping out. If people are vaccinated against **infectious** diseases, their **antibodies** will destroy **pathogens** as soon as they enter their body. This means that the pathogens have fewer opportunities to **mutate**.

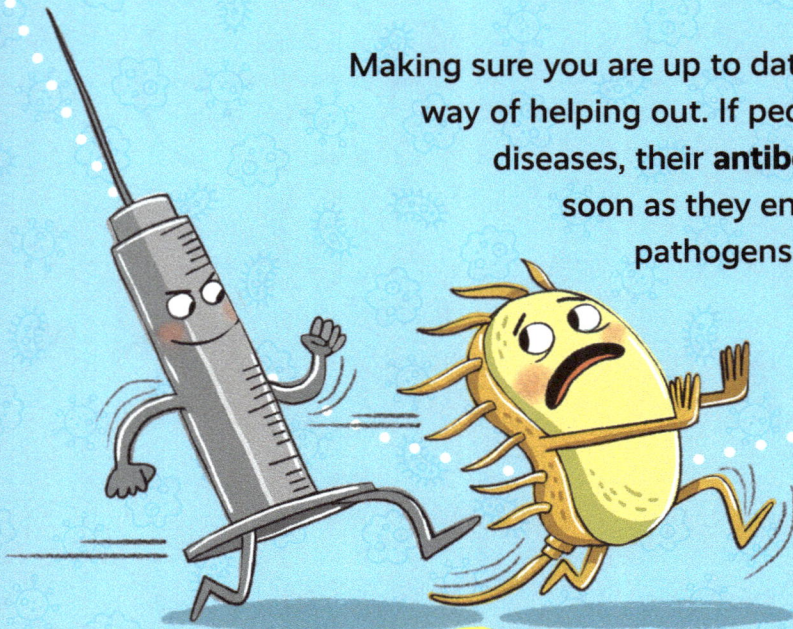

If in doubt, wash your hands! Good **hygiene** reduces the risk of picking up germs and developing an infection (which, in turn, gives the germs less of a chance to mutate!). Don't stop at hands, though—washing fruit and vegetables thoroughly before eating, cooking meat properly, only drinking clean water, and storing and reheating food correctly are also good ways of avoiding nasty germs.

Chicken needs to be cooked all the way through to make it safe to eat.

THINK ABOUT IT!

How good is your hygiene? (Be honest!) What could you do to improve it?

Improving **sanitation** around the world would also make a big difference. If waste was managed properly and wasn't left to pollute drinking water and soil, many people would avoid catching infectious diseases. Disease-resistant germs can spread around the world, so this problem affects everyone, not just the people who live there.

These children are collecting clean, treated drinking water from a well in Uganda.

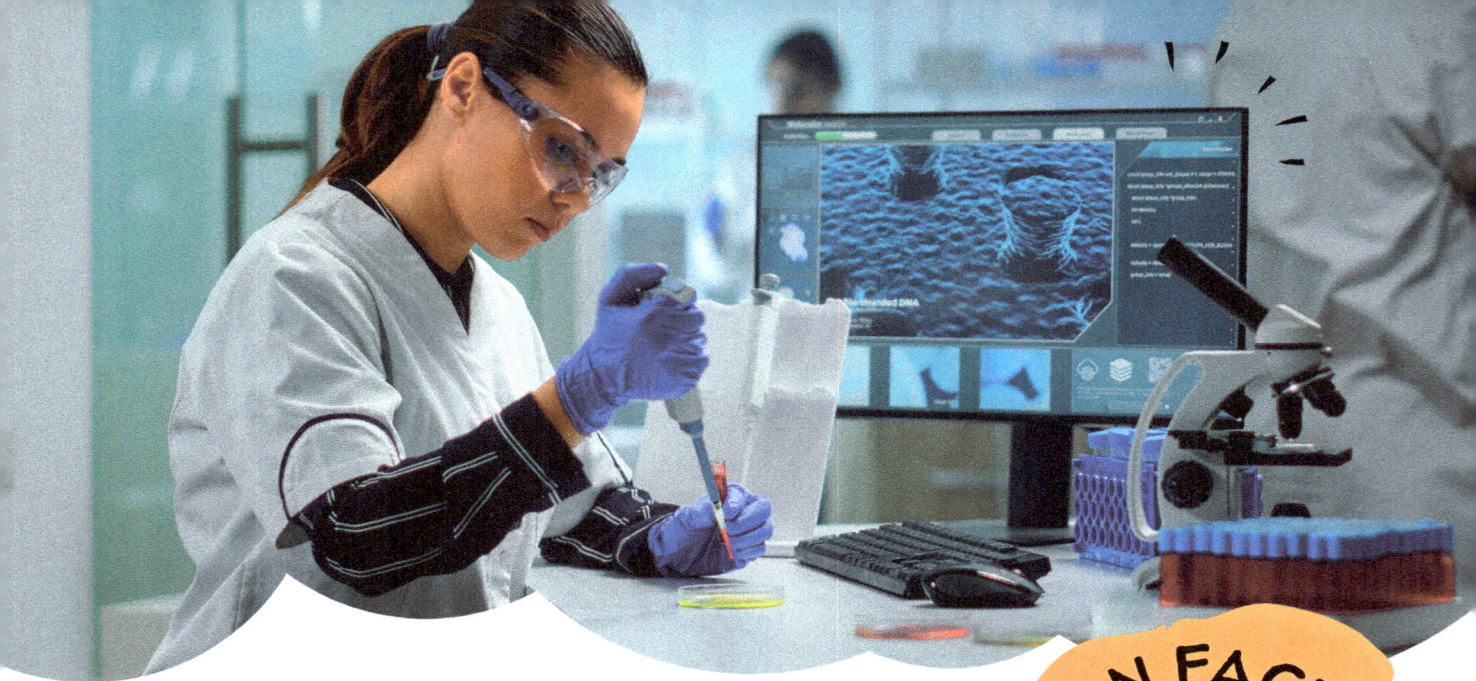

When it comes to thinking of new medicines to fight **drug**-resistant germs, human scientists are smart but slow. The solution? **Artificial intelligence** (AI)! Scientists can program an AI algorithm to scan chemicals with different antibacterial properties and suggest which ones might be effective against **superbugs.** The algorithm quickly comes up with various options, which scientists then test in a lab.

These drugs still need to be tested further before they can be widely used, but they look very promising!

This process has already helped scientists discover several new **antibiotics** that can take out drug-resistant **bacteria.** The antibiotic abaucin is effective against a superbug that causes deadly infections in hospitals. Another antibiotic called halicin works well against many different drug-resistant bacteria, including tuberculosis.

Hi! I'm Jonathan Stokes, a scientist who specializes in antibiotics. I was part of the team that discovered abaucin ... with the help of AI, of course! Artificial intelligence is such an important part of our research. It allows us to work much faster, which means we can get life-saving medicines to people even sooner. Hopefully, AI will help us find more treatments soon, so that we can make deaths from drug-resistant illnesses a thing of the past.

Thanks, buddy!

THINK ABOUT IT!

AI can be very useful, as we've seen here, but some people are worried about it replacing our jobs. What do you think?

We're here for the interview!

Conclusion

Germ-killing medicines and **vaccines** are some of the greatest inventions of the past century. They have saved thousands of millions of lives and improved the health of countless people around the world. Thanks to them, we have managed to eliminate many illnesses from certain countries and areas.

If germs became resistant to these medicines and vaccines, it would put everyone on Earth in serious danger. We would no longer be protected from such life-threatening diseases as tuberculosis or polio. Routine surgery or giving birth would put us at major risk of infection. And even a tiny cut or minor ear infection could develop into something much more unpleasant and painful without medicines to kill off nasty germs.

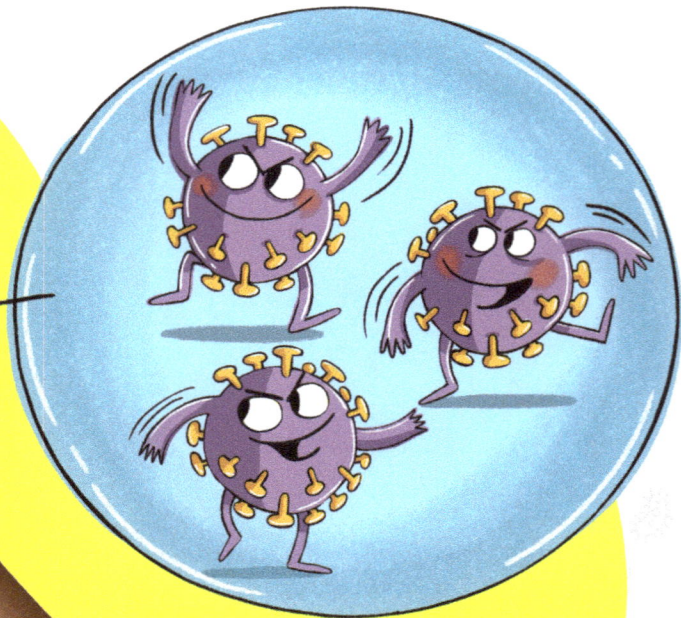

It's totally natural for germs to **mutate** and become resistant to medicine. However, there are many factors in our modern world that are making these mutations happen faster and more frequently, and these are helping **drug**-resistant germs take over. Incorrect use of medicines, overuse of medicines in farming, and poor **hygiene** and **sanitation** are all partly to blame.

FUN FACT!

The **antibiotic** penicillin has saved an estimated 200 million lives since it was first used in 1942!

However, it's not too late to make changes now that will protect life-saving medicines (and our health) for many years to come. We all have a part to play, whether that's taking medicines properly, maintaining good hygiene, or campaigning for better health care and sanitation in other parts of the world. If we all work together, we can beat these troublesome germs!

Taking the right medicine to treat your illness is important! Turn back to pages 20–21 if you don't remember why.

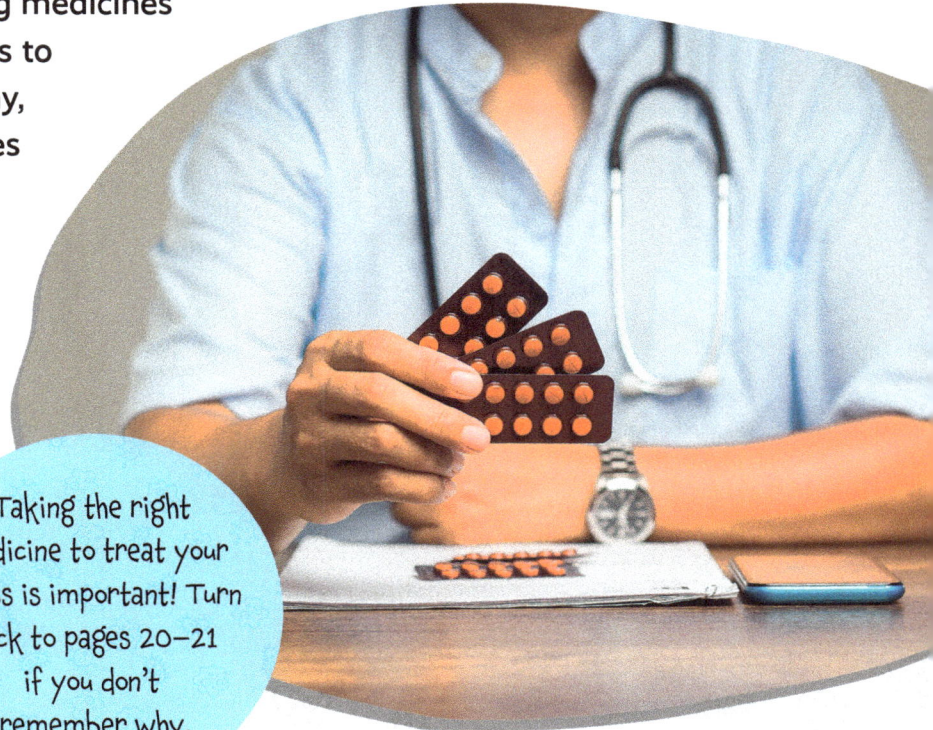

Summary

So, what would happen exactly if illnesses became resistant to medicine? Check your understanding of the information in this book.

People are taking medicines incorrectly, both the wrong type of medicine and for the wrong amount of time.

Huge quantities of medicines are given to livestock to prevent sickness.

Germs are unnecessarily exposed to medicines. Some germs are killed. A few that are naturally **drug** resistant survive.

All germs become drug resistant.

Drug-resistant germs survive and reproduce. Their population grows, and they spread from person to person, especially in areas with poor sanitation and lack of health care.

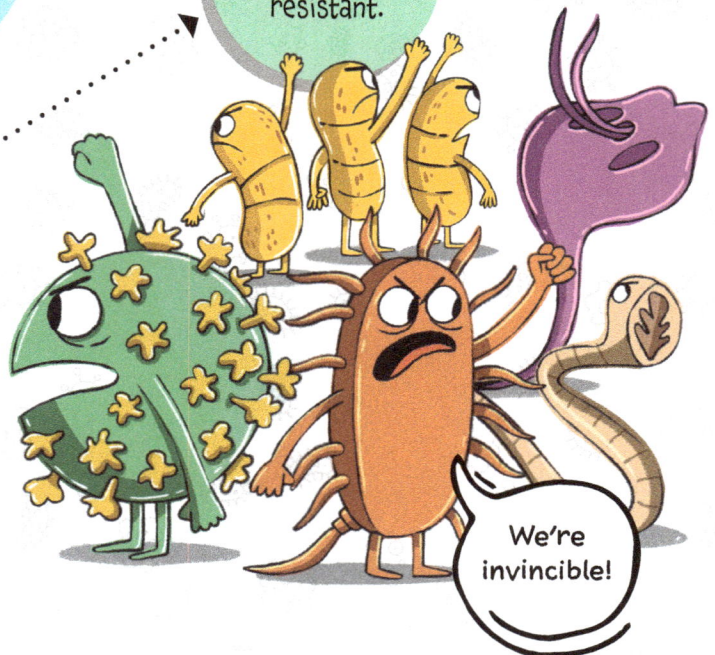

We're invincible!

Many people would catch serious infectious diseases, such as malaria and meningitis. Without treatment, they would become very sick, and many would die.

Scientists will eventually develop new medicines that work against drug-resistant germs. We'll be able to prevent and treat most infectious diseases once again.

No medicines or **vaccines** are effective against **infectious** diseases. Our **immune systems** are our only weapons against germs.

Surgery, childbirth, and chemotherapy would become much riskier without medicine to treat any infections.

THINK ABOUT IT!

Do you think it's likely that infectious illnesses will become resistant to medicine in your lifetime? Why, or why not?

Sorry, we don't have anything for that!

Glossary

airborne—an airborne illness is spread through the air

antibiotic—a medicine that can kill bacteria

antibody—a chemical that recognizes and fights germs that enter the body

antiviral—a medicine that can kill viruses

artificial intelligence (AI)—a mix of programs and data that allows computers to perform difficult tasks, such as solving problems and making decisions. Until recently, only humans were able to do this kind of "thinking."

bacterium (bacteria)—a simple living thing made up of just one cell

cell—one of the building blocks that all living things are made up of

drug—medicine

evolve—to change over time

fungus (fungi)—a small living thing that can be single- or multicelled (like mushrooms!)

gene (genes)—something found in a living thing's cells that controls its development and is passed down from its parents

hygiene—keeping yourself and your environment clean

immune system—cells and other parts of a body that protect it from disease

immunity—carrying antibodies against an illness so that you won't get sick from it again

infectious—able to be spread from person to person

infrastructure—the basic services in a country and how they are run

inherit—to be born with the same characteristics as your parents or ancestors

mutate—to randomly change and develop new characteristics

noninfectious—not able to spread from person to person

pandemic—a disease that has spread to a very wide area or almost everyone in a group of people

parasite—an animal or plant that lives on another type of animal or plant and feeds from it

pathogen—a fancy word for germ

protozoan—a single-celled living thing larger than a bacterium

reproduce—to produce young

sanitation—disposing of waste, especially from toilets

superbug—a drug-resistant germ

toxic—poisonous (watch out!)

vaccine—a substance put into a living thing's body that protects them from disease

virus—a tiny pathogen made up of particles that isn't technically alive, but can change and evolve

Review and reflect

COMPREHENSION QUESTIONS

Illness info

- What are some examples of infectious diseases?
- What are some examples of noninfectious diseases?

A world without medicine

- Without medicine, what would be our main weapon against infectious diseases? Why isn't this enough to handle all illnesses?

Mighty medicine

- How does our immune system protect us from disease?
- Why won't antibiotics help people who have a cold or the flu feel better?

Other diseases

- In general, can noninfectious illness become resistant to medicine? Why or why not?
- What is an exception to this? Explain why.

Becoming resistant

- Scientists have noticed that some medicines aren't working as effectively as they used to against infectious illnesses. Why?
- What are some factors that are making drug resistance happen faster and more often?

Fighting back

- Why should doctors be careful to prescribe medicines only when needed?
- How can artificial intelligence help scientists find more medicines to fight drug-resistant germs?

Conclusion and summary

- After reading this book and considering what would happen if illnesses became resistant to medicine, what is your biggest takeaway? Why?

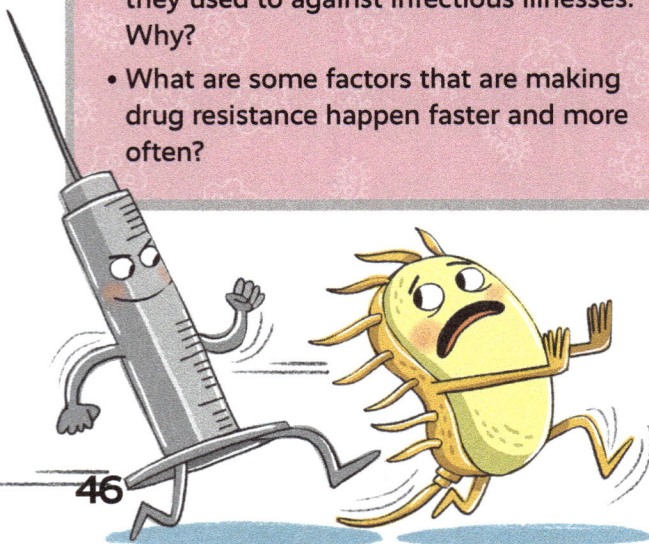

MAKE A CHAIN OF EVENTS!

Creating a paper chain can help you explore and visualize how cause and effect relationships can be thought of as a sequence of events.

You'll need:
- Pencil
- Scratch paper
- Pens or markers
- Stapler and staples
- Strips of paper
  (2 colors, if possible)

Instructions:

1. **Select a focus:** Choose a specific aspect from the book that caught your attention—it could be how people become ill or how our immune systems protect us from disease.

2. **Brainstorm causes and effects:** On a sheet of scratch paper, brainstorm and list the causes and effects related to your chosen focus. Think critically about the factors that contributed to or resulted from your focus. You can always look back in the text for ideas!

3. **Write on strips:** Write each cause and each effect on its own strip of paper. If you have different colored paper, use one color for the cause strips and the other for the effect strips.

4. **Create the paper chain:** Organize your strips into causes and effects. Start forming a paper chain to show how a cause leads to an effect. Use the stapler to connect the two strips. Continue adding cause and effect strips as links in your chain. When you've finished, you should be able to start at the beginning of your chain and read through each chain link in a logical order.

5. **Linking multiple chains:** If your focus has multiple causes or effects, you can create additional chains and link them together to show how complex cause and effect relationships can be!

Write about it!

Look at the paper chain you created and how the causes link to effects (which in turn link to other causes!). How might breaking a link in the chain impact the overall sequence of events?

World Book, Inc.
180 North LaSalle Street
Suite 900
Chicago, Illinois 60601
USA

For information about other World Book publications, visit our website at www.worldbook.com or call 1-800-WORLDBK (967-5325).

For information about sales to schools and libraries, call 1-800-975-3250 (United States), or 1-800-837-5365 (Canada).

Library of Congress Control Number: 2024941781

What Would Happen If...
ISBN: 978-0-7166-7125-1 (set, hard cover)

Illnesses Became Resistant to Medicine?
ISBN: 978-0-7166-7128-2 (hard cover)
ISBN: 978-0-7166-7140-4 (e-book)
ISBN: 978-0-7166-7134-3 (soft cover)

Staff

Editorial

Vice President
Tom Evans

Editorial Project Coordinator
Kaile Kilner

Curriculum Designer
Caroline Davidson

Senior Editor
Shawn Brennan

Proofreader
Nathalie Strassheim

Graphics and Design

Senior Visual
Communications Designer
Melanie Bender

Digital Asset Specialist
Rosalia Bledsoe

Written by Izzi Howell
Illustrated by Paula Bossio

Developed with World Book by White-Thomson Publishing LTD

Acknowledgments

4-5 © Melinda Nagy, Shutterstock; © AtlasStudio/Shutterstock
6-7 © Bencemor/Shutterstock
8-9 © Ashley Cooper pics/Alamy Images; © Me dia/Shutterstock
10-11 © charnw/Shutterstock; © Dr Morley Read, Shutterstock
12-13 © PR Image Factory/Shutterstock; © Science Picture Co/Alamy Images
14-15 © loocmill/Shutterstock; © dpa picture alliance/Alamy Images
16-17 © Xinhua/Alamy Images; © Ashley Cooper pics/Alamy Images
18-19 © Thaiview/Shutterstock; © Towfiqu ahamed barbhuiya/Shutterstock
20-21 © Purple Clouds/Shutterstock; © Zaharia Bogdan Rares, Shutterstock
22-23 © agefotostock /Alamy Images; © Ewa Studio/Shutterstock
24-25 © 15Studio/Shutterstock; © andriano.cz/Shutterstock
26-27 © Jake Lyell, Alamy Images; © Juice Verve/, hutterstock
28-29 © Ian Dagnall Computing/Alamy Images; © Yusnizam Yusof, Shutterstock
30-31 © Tyler Olson, Shutterstock; © A.Azarnikova/Shutterstock
32-33 © Toa55/Shutterstock; © Pixel-Shot/Shutterstock
34-35 © Prostock-studio/Shutterstock; © Artem Evdokimov, Shutterstock
36-37 © Timolina/Shutterstock; © mohammad arar/Alamy Images
38-39 © DC Studio/Shutterstock; © New Africa/Shutterstock
40-41 © meeboonstudio/Shutterstock; © MIA Studio/Shutterstock